Polk Street

San Francisco

by
Serena Czarnecki

Illustrations and Photography by R.A. Morgan
Cover and Interior design by Vinnie Corbo

Volossal
Publishing

Published by Volossal Publishing
www.volossal.com

Copyright © 2021
ISBN 978-1-7350184-8-5

Dedication

For Lucy,
the Diamond of my eye

and

for Morgan
the only man smart enough to give me Chanel No.22

Polk Street

After the assignations and tumult of the 1960's, after the Hippy Movement stopped a War, after the deluge.

Crazy things were still happening in the 1970's. I was living in San Francisco during the middle of that decade. I was married and had been living in Los Angeles, making money through nude modeling which led to erotic film work. My husband and I would do the magazine modeling together at first, though we always seemed to be fighting at home.

When I first began in this underground world I was very young and shy. Not shy of my body, I'd been taught that the nude form is beautiful, but shy of strangers. I'd not had much experience with any grown men, and didn't know the photographers.

I'd come to get along great with the photographers, as I became quite popular as a model and in demand. But when starting out, I worried about what my husband would think, and liked him on set for my protection. Sometimes he'd don a short-hair wig and pose with me.

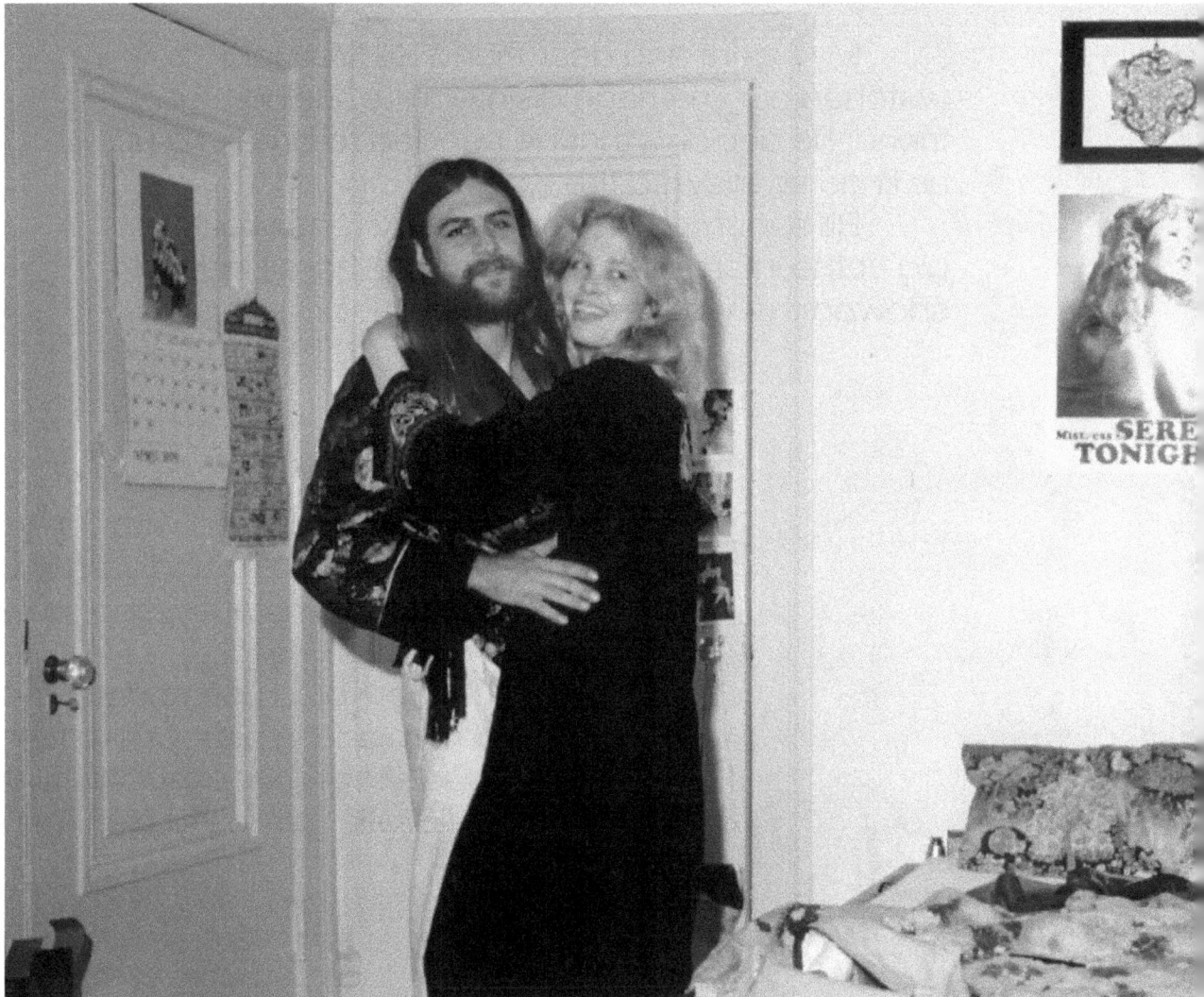

My first husband had long, long hair which we considered his freak flag. His long hair defined him then and still does. He smoked a lot of weed and we took LSD together. The good trips were great for me. He did put me through some really difficult trips, however -- I think he just enjoyed playing mind games. So my bad trips were very bad and I needed to go through Linguistic Programming to rid myself of them.

My Agent and dear friend Bill Margold watched our marriage disintegrate. Being a good friend, he decided that he needed to break us up, as I had swallowed the Kool-Aid.

Bill sent me to New York City for a week's gig at the infamous Show World, where I indeed showed the world everything!

I worked onstage with Joey Silvera and met Vanessa Del Rio and Jamie. Jamie Gillis conquered me instantly, and the week turned into two years.

Jamie would use and abuse me, but with charm and in play. Unlike first Husband, who was altogether unsophisticated in the ways of Erotic games of Dominance.

Jamie Gillis

Eventually I needed to leave New York, I was missing California, my home. In all of Central Park there wasn't enough green.

I had to leave Jamie, but he ended up following me.

        I never thought it was a successful transplant, Jamie was NY through and through, born and raised. He came out to visit me. We attended a Renaissance Faire in the woods of Marin County and then visited my sister who was caring for my child.

I've always regretted not seeing Lucy's first steps, but my sister, who was also with me at the birth, did. My sister would support me and fight with me when First Husband took me to Custody Court. She was Super Aunt to my baby, and when my child grew older she'd have my other sister to see after her too.

Seeing my sisters at Lucy's wedding is one of the highlights of my life. We all looked fabulous, Darling! The bride shining like a Diamond. Though her new husband is an incredible chef, the reception was catered, and the food was yummy. It was a themed wedding and their children were dressed in 1920s style. Lucy's son started dancing and never stopped, as long as we were there! Her daughter was so grown-up and stunning, at first I didn't recognize her! Kids grow fast when you can only see them every year or so.

My sister had moved with her husband to "The Land" after my baby was born in Santa Cruz. So there we were. Jamie in his leather hand-sewn top-hat that he'd purchased at the Faire back in Marin, and I, visiting The Land. And First Husband came to see us, naked with boots on, from his neighboring Land - for which I had paid with modeling money.

Of course a little nudity wasn't going to phase Jamie Gillis, the Prince of Porn.

First Husband and I went to junior high school together, dated, fucked, and did drugs together. I was already in and out of my parent's by the time I was in Middle School, usually going to stay with my sister and her husband. But he needed to run away from home to get his freedom. His adoptive folks were strict in their religious beliefs, none of which he or I agreed.

We smoked weed for recreation, but LSD was the drug of choice to expand our minds. You could be on LSD and know things in the most profound way, knowledge you could take with you into your everyday life. I'm sure that these trips taught me things so deeply that I've been able to understand things in my life immediately. I just seem to know something fully, understand it, without explanation. LSD provided me with sight. Large vision.

Most trips were fun, but a few were horrible. The worst acid trip I experienced was when First Husband and I were in his station wagon. Eventually we lived in that vehicle. This night we were still dating.

We made love (high on LSD), what I most loved doing - especially on LSD! I recall lying beneath him in the long bed of the car. As I climaxed a million white doves began to flap their wings and I could hear hymns. Ecstasy! Then, he took me outside, sat me on the hood, and showed me that our hometown was burning. Flames seemed to be eating all the places I dearly loved. Because of the warm Santa Ana winds, La Crescenta would get an almost yearly fire season, but I've never been able to tell if any of this was real, or First Husband's sick way of manipulating me.

Years later, during Neuro-linguistic Programming (NLP) Seminars, I was asked to make the burning town appear as if on a huge movie screen. I was to pretend to sit in a theater seat and watch the horror over and over again until it didn't hurt any more. Then I could shrink it to pea size gradually and let it dissolve. I was able to let go of the hurtfulness of this memory in this way.

I first took acid with First Husband, and I took acid for the last time when living with Jamie Gillis in a hotel in San Francisco. Jamie saved me by helping me through the bad part of the trip. He took me to the Fern Garden. And though that trip ended beautifully, I never took the drug again. I'd seen enough to hold me my lifetime.

While Jamie saved me by helping me through a bad trip, my New York friend, who knew nothing of drugs, would take me to Golden Gate Park. There I experienced the growing things and luckily my bad trip smoothed out to become beautiful.

SERENA CZARNECKI

I went with my junior high school friend, First Husband, when he ran away to Berkeley. We collected spare change for the Free Clinic, ate free meals in a Unitarian Church (even ate moose there!), and lived in the station wagon. Then his parents found us in Oregon through the Police. We'd gotten jobs picking pears in a huge orchard and were happy.

Caught, he spent time in Juvenile Hall and was then put in a Half-Way House. He could go out in the daytime but had to sleep under supervision. I moved close by. That's how we ended up in the San Fernando Valley. In this wide valley north of Hollywood, the nudie magazines of the day were published.

Never being ashamed to show off my beautiful body, I was a hit as a model! I made some XXX rated films and then we retired to the country. The money I'd made paid for the down payment on Land (40 acres) near my sister, on Crooked Prairie, Northern California.

My friend Bill Margold, who also acted as my Agent his whole life, had sent me to NYC to get me away from my toxic marriage. I ended up staying, having fallen in deep Lust with Jamie Gillis. Both Jamie and our "slave" Ebon would join me and my first husband at the Polk Street place!

Ebon was a sweet young Puerto Rican who adored Jamie and would do anything for him. Jamie picked him up on a street in "Hell's Kitchen" and brought him to our apartment in New York to have sex. Jamie needed his balls licked while fucking me.

Ebon would run our errands and became indispensable. He was quiet and nice, good-looking - just a sweet youth. I cannot remember names, so end up calling folks by names I think suit them. I named this young man "Ebony" and he was thereafter known as "Ebon."

In California, he walked up Polk Street to buy me a CD of music he thought I'd like. His present would delight me. He turned me on to the B-52s! I really dug them and their song *Love Shack* would be a part of my future. My family would name their lake house "Love Shack" on Put-In-Bay back east.

On Land (40 acres) near my sister, miles from nowhere, First Husband and I had lived off wild berries until my breast milk ran blue! The Spring water kept the beer cold. I loved our baby more than life itself, so excited to see her discover something new each day. She was carried next to my heart in a pouch, we were still as one being.

When pregnant I was fulfilled, full of joy, full with child, filled with the possibilities of the future. Although I did have a bit of morning sickness at first, it never got me down - afterwords I'd feel fine and have a happy day. I was more happy when pregnant than I ever have been. It was wonderful getting "fat."

Lucy and I seemed to communicate while she was yet in the womb. I can recall the exact moment she was conceived! First husband and I were enjoying sex on the floor of our apartment in the Valley, high on LSD. (No furniture because we were always poor.) In my mind's eye I saw the sperm swim up my tube, meet an egg and WOW! I had the beginning of life in my body. I could see it. I knew at once this union would produce a female.

We named her Lucy Sky Diamond in honor of that moment. She has been the "diamond of my eye" - the reason my eyes twinkle.

Her father threatened to name the baby Lucifer Space Dragon if it was a boy, but I always knew my baby would grow to be a girl child. I do love Lucy!

On *my* birth certificate under place of birth, "none" is typed in. (?) Maybe I was a miracle and wasn't born at all? Actually, I think that's there because they didn't know how to express that I was born under an oak tree.

On Lucy's birth certificate I wrote out "Lucy in the Sky with Diamonds" as her name! I was so blissed-out when she was born I could barely think straight!

My euphoria would be long-lasting. Giving birth is a sacred deed and I've worshiped at the Altar of Life ever since. However, depression from my disorder would conflict with my optimism in grave ways...

"the diamond of my eye..."

First Husband and I fought all the time. We were in competition and neither of us were good losers. We never learned to be an adult couple. We were forever teenagers with no clue. I needed to get away from him and went to my sister's place in Santa Cruz to have the baby.

My beautiful red-headed sister was with me during the birthing. I was looking in her eyes as Lucy came into this world. "Welcome," I said.

I was alone with my precious newborn for a month because I'd had to get away from First Husband. Again.

Soon after my sister moved with her husband to The Land in northern California. Lucy and I visited them when they were still living in a tipi as he was building their home. It was a very livable abode, that tipi, I'm used to sitting on the floor. We'd sit on rugs around the central fire and my sister would make her delicious food. The land was away from civilization - golden rolling hills, spectacular views and very peaceful.

Before they left Santa Cruz, they set me up in a little cottage with a rocking chair. I nursed my tiny baby while rocking and was completely content. One evening however, as I was going to visit my sister, I tripped and fell over a jagged, broken piece of sidewalk. We both fell. As I felt my skinned knee, I heard a deathly silence. My heart stopped to listen. It was the most scary silence I had ever heard. Finally Lucy began screaming and I was so relieved.

Later, when First Husband and I were renting a shack with a separate Tower out on The Land, the baby would fall from her bed. (My little sister fell from her bed too. I remember that night clearly. There is an awful uproar when a baby falls.)

We took Lucy to the hospital in the small town near The Land. Her head was X-rayed and they found two hairline injuries to her sweet head, so Social Services got involved. A nice man paid us a visit to discuss the safe ways to handle a child. I recall speaking with him while stirring rags in an outdoor tub boiling on the wood-stove. The rags were used as her diapers.

We found land to buy and moved onto an empty piece. It was ours and it had a small creek. It's flow wasn't strong enough to run a generator, however, but we had water. The dream was "forty acres and a mule." We had the forty acres! We set up a tent and an open sky and fresh air greeted us each AM. First Husband would light up a doobie while still half asleep and the smoke would drive me out into the morning chill.

One day at the Post Office in town I received a telegram! This was totally unexpected - I didn't know that anybody even knew where I was! I thought I had disappeared, retired from The Biz. I wanted a life with my lovely daughter and a garden. The telegram was from Jim and Artie Mitchell offering me a job. They would entice me back to the spotlight. Some things in my life come "from out of the blue," like this telegram, and things from the "blue" usually change the path of my steps.

First Husband now needed money for wood so he could build us a house. We packed up our panel truck and headed south to The City by The Bay, San Francisco, with our daughter. We parked in an underground parking garage, leaving the baby snuggled in the laundry in the back of the truck. We really weren't old enough, mature enough, and drugged too often to have any sense. We went across the street to the O'Farrell Theatre to meet with the Mitchells. The brothers met with us, then handed us off to a tech to show us around. There were various venues of adult entertainment in the theatre.

The sound/light engineer turned me onto The Talking Heads, and we were instant pals. (My Dad would say that David Byrne is a genius. Dad knew one when he saw one!)

What I saw in the Ultra Room was a bit shocking, but mostly a turn-on. Three girls were in black studded leather, lingerie and nude. The entire room was upholstered in black leather, including the ceiling and a buoyant floor. There was a trapeze bar from which to swing. A lady would hang from it upside-down and the other two women would lick her pussy.

They spanked one another and laughed and giggled and seemed to be having a great time. There were mirrors all around the room. The technician took us to the "backstage" area. The mirrors were two-way and men could buy tickets to view the Ultra action. They were either standing in a gallery or they could buy a private room.

I wouldn't want to be the person to clean up those private rooms!

I would eventually work inside this room, making many great friends, making love to these girl friends.

There was also a Main Stage where Headliners would put on a dance strip show.

Marilyn Chambers was the Headliner quite often. She could sing and dance and really put on a show. The brothers made good deals with her to Star in their films and the three of them would play cards late into the night. Now the Mitchell brothers wanted me to come out of retirement to Headline.

They would put a big advertisement in the San Francisco paper announcing me. It was such good money. Since I could work at many of the rooms at the O'Farrell, I ended up getting my own flat up the street: Polk Street.

We dubbed the big corner theatre "The Fish Tank" because then the whole building was beautifully painted with a mural depicting underwater life - including a whale!

I never did get cozy with the brothers. They were "The Bosses." Artie seemed sweet. Jim had a mean edge and they both did way too much cocaine.

So First Husband would end up staying on The Land while I worked (and played) in The City. It was a taste of freedom for me. The first apartment (we called them flats) I had with a lease in my name. I had to pay rent and be a big girl. I was elated. It was a huge step in my becoming free. Free to do as I pleased, lived like I wanted and think my own thoughts. Freedom to be a responsible human would need years and medications to help me. Freedom to be whole, without the distractions of self-pity and/or terror of failure. Freedom to grow up!

I could walk to work at the O'Farrell Theatre, just six short blocks to Polk and O'Farrell Streets. Polk Street was a mostly Gay area so I felt safe (I was usually tarted up). The shops and restaurants up and down the hill beckoned. I felt independent, but of course missed my daughter terribly. I gained roommates as time went on, and Lucy would come to live with us. I even got a male Nanny for her. (He cared for my little girl, but also tended me. I was still at loose-ends, but getting better all the time.)

I'd hang out in the bar at The Palms Cafe downstairs, ordering Blue Moons because I liked the name. They were a mixed drink. At home I'd keep a bottle of Jack Daniels to sip or slug. I sat in a cherished red leather, wing-backed chair that was in the den/dining room where I'd drink my Jack. A big dining table and chairs were there.

Annette Haven, Lysa Adams, Tiffany Clark and I would color eggs with Lucy on it. Morgan would take pictures of us. Each Spring I color eggs in celebration of the Equinox. I got so much joy sharing this with my little daughter. We had SO much fun! We colored dozens and dozens of eggs. The boiling pots in the kitchen steamed up the windows.

(see photo on page 9)

I drank too much. I was self-medicating my bipolar disease. I was still not diagnosed, and medications were far in my future. Every day my life was a tale of compensating for my disorder. Drinking alcohol was my way of dealing with my problem. My topsy-turvy life consisted of sexual mania, buying sprees, and staying awake for days on end...

or

...in the depths of depression - sleeping, crying, hiding, sleeping, weeping, sleeping, sobbing.

I'd been in this state since a teenager, having fits or contemplating suicide. Having no idea what was wrong with me until a doctor prescribed lithium for me when in my late twenties. It took marrying again and moving to Florida to find this doctor. I'd been misdiagnosed in my teens and had suffered much because of that.

First Husband came down from The Land to build me a huge bed frame, a box that he could stash his "Grow" within. Garbage bags of weed were under my mattress. He brought his then-girlfriend, Siva. She hadn't worn shoes in decades. Her dirty feet didn't bother me...she bothered me! She was a Devil Worshiper and her idol was Charles Manson. While in San Francisco she'd go to San Quentin Prison every day in hopes of getting an audience with Charlie.

Charles Manson scared me until the day he finally died. He took my childhood from me. The country lost its innocence with the killing of JFK, but Murdering Manson stole any hopes of continuing my happy childhood. Tiny Siva left her Magic Pouch on my bookcase, telling me not to touch it. She said it held dead kittens. I was happy when she left my flat.

In the strange year of 2020, our Fearful President would Post a picture of himself on Twitter looked over by an "Angel"; Charlie Manson. This brought up all the horror again! Knowing about the Hindu Goddess Kali and being in a Death Cult are very different things.

Jamie came out to be in a movie and stayed with me. Officially we were "still together," but while I had a grand time with him in New York City, I was different in my home state. I was back to being a California Girl. The dirtiness of Manhattan was just a memory and so was my lust for Jamie. He was so damn charming though, that when he wanted to try out the West Coast who was I to say no? I did "sleep" with him on occasion, but he had his own room. I took the main living area as my bedroom all to myself with my huge bed; a California King.

Sometimes I'd try my hand at painting and I considered it my Studio. But the call of dancing and being a Sex Goddess was stronger than paint! Then. Paint would pull me back to the worship of Art later in my life.

L to R: Tiffany Clark, Lysa Adams and friend.

Working at the Mitchell Brother's Theatre pretty frequently, I began to bring my work home with me. I'd bring home girls I favored to party! And Jamie was always one to seduce them. Soon there was a path from the Theatre to his penis! I joined him and Lysa Adams in sex and ended up "giving" her to him as his slave-girl. She was submissive in bed. I wanted her to be my cook, but she'd spend most of her time in Jamie's room. I could hear her sex screams down the hall.

A young woman I "worked" with was infatuated with me - she would do anything, do everything for me. She became a pest, wanting to be my slave, needing more and more of my attention. She was convinced that I was absolutely perfect. She'd follow me home from The O'Farrell and wouldn't leave me. She refused to leave my house. She was fun to have sex with at work, even a good addition to my Salons, but she became tiresome. Too much for me to handle.

One evening I was drunk and she kept holding a piece of broken mirror up to my face.

"Look at yourself!" she cried out. "You are perfection. You are so gorgeous!"

Being manic and frustrated with her nonsense, I grabbed the shard of mirror glass and raked my calf with it.

"No! No! No! See, I'm NOT perfect - I bleed!"

I just remember seeing her head go down to lick my leg wound before I really started screaming at her to get the fuck out. That scratch I gave myself turned into a reminder-scar. Slaves can be a real bore.

Morgan was my next Best Thing. I'd been abused by relationships. Battered down by arguments with First Husband, S&M with Jamie. Jamie suited my NY self. He represented all the taxi drivers jerking off looking in their rear-views at me. I fell in love and lust with Morgan. He felt clean...like California. I was a blonde Sunshine Girl. He could have been my blonde surf boy.

First Husband smelled of Skunk Weed. Jamie smelled like his awful cigars. Morgan smelled like sun-dried sheets to me.

Morgan didn't walk, he danced in his Capezio slippers. When we promenaded down Polk, he took leaps over each parking meter. I admired his agility. I was always a bit clumsy. He was a Pierrot. He was entranced by the character. His bed-sheets were covered with illustrations of Pierrot. Pierrot masks were in his room. To me, Morgan was Classical Music, First Husband loud Hard Rock, Jamie the sound from a smokey corner bar.

I met this beautiful man on a set of a "loop." He was my partner and we gleefully fucked away an afternoon. I was XXXtremely turned on, more than on other sets. He was gorgeous and I wanted to screw his brains out! By the end of that day, I hadn't gotten enough of him. So we went back to my Polk Street flat to continue to paw, kiss and handle each other. I'd never brought anyone home from a set before and I didn't want him to leave.

And he didn't! He went back to his place and packed up and came to live with me. From that moment I felt my life had been blessed. Not only was he a great roommate, he'd become a good friend to me. We separated to live our lives, but I'd continue loving him over the years. I often dreamed of him. I felt reassured when he came to me in a dream. He was still looking after me.

It was this deep commitment that got me through some hard times. I knew he was out there somewhere and he was my friend.

At the flat, girls would cum and come and go, thanks to Jamie's sexual appetite. Many would visit from the theatre down the block. So many that I began having Salons: Wednesday, Friday, Saturday Night Salons.

Salons - I can't remember what day, but folks came. The girls would bring other girls or their boyfriends and my house would be full. Sometimes they'd splinter off to make Jamie happy in his room. We'd drink, laugh, smoke and talk about nothing and everything, playing music loud. We'd stand at the Bay windows to gaze at the lit street and wave at people as they walked by - sometimes even asking them up if they looked interesting.

We'd drink wine and Jack and smoke pot. Cocaine became the rage of the day and people would share it. I always kept a rolled-up hundred dollar bill with which to snort it.

I loved to dance and perform. I enjoyed making movies. In those days, we were actually trying to make movies - with sex in them.

Alas, this never caught on, so the 1970s remain a special moment in film history. I was glad to be a part of it. Although I'm glad to be out of it too.

Now I have the time to create - art. I use the medias of sculpture, paintings, mono-types, silkscreens, block prints, line drawings and pastels. I have written books and have hooked rugs. I have also crocheted and braided rugs. Some of my work is erotic, most is not.

"In my day," the 1970s, the actors were my Jamie, John Leslie, Joey Silvera, John Seeman and John Holmes of course. Holmes, with his enormous dick, was the King. Johnny Wad. I considered Jamie to be the Prince of Porn. Seka, Annette Haven and I were contemporaries. Annette actually had her own house just up the way, off Polk. She and her roommate Blair would visit me. (I'd met Blair on a set and he was also a lover of mine.) First Husband would become her friend (and Lover, I assumed.) She would become obsessed with Lucy and would take on the role of her "mother" at Lucy's first wedding. I was a guest only.

Goddess, would I end up dreading Annette. She would post negative things about me for years on her Social Media. My Fans would report it to me. I let her slip from my mind. My revenge is not thinking about her.

Annette was very beautiful. Pale skin and long straight dark hair, just First Husband's type. She seemed stand-offish to me, though we made films together. She gave an excellent performance in *Dracula Sucks* - the role Gillis was born to play. But when my dear Morgan got his camera, Annette was a willing model. She and I would pose together for his lens, creating wonderful shots together with my daughter. My roommate Lysa Adams would also pose, and Tiffany Clark and Jamie too.

One day making pictures, I told Annette and Morgan about my idea for a Solstice gift for Lucy's Dad. With their urging, I decided to stage the photo.

First Husband and I were into Rock Music. He considered guitarist Ritchie Blackmore of Deep Purple a God. I also listened to that band, and when needing to use a false name for Playboy's *OUI Magazine*, I choose Ian Gillian's last name. (Magazines at the time would give the models false names and make up stories about them. For *OUI Magazine*, I was Jenn Gillian. It wasn't until I became known in films that Serena, my real name, would get used. Sexy Serena!

Ian was Jesus in the *Jesus Christ: Superstar* recording, and the singer for Deep Purple.

We liked other rock too, and while living on Polk Street, The Tubes were a favorite. First Husband and I even saw them locally at The Greek Theater. One of The Tubes songs spoke of a baby's arm holding an apple. As I set the scene to illustrate this song, Annette freshened Lulu's make-up and Morgan adjusted the lights. I found an old baby doll and took it's arm and an apple from the fruit bowl to the set.

I sat spread-eagle on the floor in front of Morgan's tripod and inserted the doll arm into my vagina. I set the apple just out of it's reach. It did, indeed, look to be reaching for the apple. We took a few shots, Annette laughing, directing. I was getting along with First Husband at that time and was excited to provide him with a photo I knew he'd love. Lucy sat behind me for a couple of shots. All in all, everyone had a great day modeling for our beloved Morgan's lens.

Morgan having a camera was a super turn-on for me. I pretended to be a young Marilyn Monroe, posing for cover after cover. There was nothing I found more thrilling than being followed around by a camera. Picture taking was in my blood. My father made me his model when I was quite young and my brother would become a professional photographer. Later, while living in Miami, Florida I was to make money photographing "Head Shots" for up-and-coming models.

There was a thriving fashion industry there at the time. Agencies and models were always in need of photos and portfolios and I was decent at taking pictures. In Florida there was plenty of available light! A photographer I knew in my early modeling days taught First Husband and I to develop film in our tiny bathroom in The Valley.

For a time, First Husband and I partnered in a sort of model referral agency at that apartment we called Fox Office. At the Art Center in Florida I set up a Darkroom for all to use.

I adored Morgan and the photos he took were an expression of true art. His photos were my expression of true love for him and for what we created. He would draw expertly.

I was a little jealous of his amazing talent. But I could be there for his camera. That was how I created beauty in those days. I needed to get out of The Biz to find my true self as an artist. My Second Husband would provide me with a Studio in which to paint and bought me literally gallons of oil paint - mixed up for me special.

Morgan became a very true friend to me, besides being a fantastic lover. He helped to tend my child, Lucy. I loved her more than anything on the planet, but wasn't really sure how to care for her. I had a younger sister, but we weren't allowed to be with one another due to my bipolar condition. My mother separated us because I could be violent. I knew nothing about how to act with kids. The people I admired and hung out with were my teachers and people older than myself.

Morgan was a nice person and therefore just fun to be around. Jamie was dark, a beast with charm. First Husband and I were locked in space battling together. I have had to become nice as I age. I don't think I'm naturally nice at all. I've had to fight through my depression and mania since being a little girl and it toughened me. It made me hard and bossy. My first instinct to protect myself is to lash out in anger. Even now with the help of meds, if you ask me a question, any question, my answer is "No." Even if I mean "Yes." I will answer "No, I mean yes."

This may all be imprinted on me from birth, who knows? As my mom and I were in a hospital bed together, my dear dad brought us a birthing present in a big pink box - boxing gloves! Dad had assumed his first child would be a boy. Maybe this is why I've always been feisty. But I am also generous, more than happy to share my toys!

Lysa Adams/Thatcher was a docile person - very sweet, level-headed and pretty. She was a quiet person and didn't interfere with my demands. Bossy as a kid, I was a born leader. Leader of my pack.

I liked Lysa a lot, especially for taking over my Jamie "duties." Jamie was not a great transplant to the lifestyle of California, although I know he had fun with all the new flesh to fuck. He was a New Yorker through and through and I was happy for him when he returned there.

I would see him years later. My Second Husband would take him out for sushi. We also spoke over the phone at the last place he would live. He died of lung cancer and his obituary would be in newspapers across the nation. I'm grateful for our time together.

Our flat was one of two in a San Francisco style dwelling. I don't think our gay neighbors liked us much. I heard them call us "Breeders" under their breath. And I'm sure we made too much noise during the Salons. But I couldn't be happier than in a predominately gay neighborhood. I'd had too much of straight men grabbing at me, pinching me, saying foul things to me. I loved putting on make-up and dressing up, but don't you know that women dress for each other? We do not dress to get attention from men. The whistles and jeers are unwelcome.

The neighborhood consisted of low buildings with restaurants and shops on the ground level. It was quaint. Houses were painted in many colors, California style, and though similar in architecture, each was unique. The street was sloping, as most in The City, but not steep. Easy to walk to my favorite bookstore, the shop I bought Lucy's pretty dresses and Swan's Oyster Depot where I drank champagne and ate caviar.

I was into Aleister Crowley. I was very good at throwing Tarot cards and his deck was something I absolutely depended on every day. My sister collected Tarot decks and I made a series of oil paintings that were my version of each card. My "Big Women" series.

I've seen and used many decks over the years, but the Thoth deck is still my favorite. I do not throw every day anymore, but feel they are a good guide and teaching tool. At the bookstore across Polk Street I purchased Crowley's entire encyclopedia of Magick, wisdom and utter nonsense.

Not knowing how to get Lucy to settle down for sleep, I read to her out of these books - hoping my droning voice would send her off to Dreamland. Morgan was much better at getting her to go to sleep in her back-porch bedroom. My black cat would roam the rooftops out there.

Lucy had been naked most of her life. First Husband said it would make her strong. I don't know how many times I heard, "Isn't that baby cold?" from passers-by, but she'd run around naked in all sorts of weather and not be cold. She never caught a cold. Native Americans would strip off what they wore when it rained. Much better to feel the droplets than get your clothes soaking wet. Clothes were a burden, something to care for, so many Natives shed them in order to move freely. California Native Americans just stayed inside when it rained, as do I.

Tiffany Clark

I did love taking Lulu up the street to the children's dress shop. She could have anything she wanted and I spoiled her with pretty dresses, frilly underwear, ankle sox and patent leather shoes. I loved to buy such items for her daughter, and my Grandchild, later. It would be my Grandchild who wore my First Communion Dress from my Catholic childhood - she would wear it to High Tea! I was so proud to have passed along something from my youth. I'll never forget training for, and the day of, my First Communion. It's a big deal, not only do you partake of the wafer and wine (grape juice) ritual, but you get a special white fancy dress, like a bride. (In my late twenties, I would convert to be a Jew. My Rabbi Rami Shapiro would take Lucy to tour Israel.)

Working The O'Farrell Theatre

Ultra Room

Favorite songs in The Ultra Room were anything by The Talking Heads or Marvin Gaye. *Witchy Woman* was a mainstay of mine to strip to and *Another One Bites the Dust* was fun for bondage shows. I also liked a song by Marianne Faithful which talked of her little "oyster."

Getting ready upstairs, backstage, we ladies stared into the room-length mirror, applying more and more make-up, talking to each other's reflection. Smoke would raise from always-full ashtrays as our lipstick got more and more red.

Most of the girls were talkative. They spoke of their parents, their boyfriends, having sex with their boyfriend, fights with their boyfriends, fighting with their parents, and getting high. Talk was also about the customers' rudeness, though at that I had to laugh - we *were* there pushing our pussies in their faces!

The long hours, doing many shows, one every half an hour, got to be wearisome. We were all bone-tired by the end of our shift. Ah, the allure of Show Biz.

We'd rouse ourselves to get up to perform. We'd run down the stairs and explode into the all-black room. We'd continue talking and the talk would get sexual quickly. There'd be cat-of-nine tail whips, crops and dildos laying about - to pick up and use on thighs, breasts, butts and pussies. We would go around the room showing off our leather or lingerie-clad bodies while holding our nipples and squeezing our titties. Telling the other girls how nice their tits were, wanting to compare and feel another women's breasts.

Couples would form, first with one and then another, to disperse and we'd gaze intently at the two-way mirrors. Trust me, the men on the other side of those mirrors got their money's worth! Every show in the Ultra Room would leave the women sweaty and used up.

I'd hoist myself onto the hanging bar in the black leather room and hang by my knees. The others would take turn licking my button, driving me wild. If I didn't cum several times with the girls, I wasn't having a good time, not doing a good show. We all were seriously wanting to pleasure the others. I'd have my butt whipped while my slit was being tongued. My shy nipple would be sucked until it made an appearance. I would groan in delight and the girls would try to outdo each other, wanting to make me scream!

We'd all dance to the piped-in music, coming together to grope and grab and kiss. We'd rub our crotches on another's knee as we danced, laughing, having a great time. My favorite woman to engage with in the Ultra Room was Tanya. She always wore a colorful turban, I have no idea what her hair was like. Tanya would rub almond oil over her exquisite body, smelled like almonds, was the color of smoked almonds. She was gorgeous, lots of fun. I loved her, but only once did she visit me at home and I took some photos of her.

We played at the theatre but it was only Wicked Wanda that I made friends with outside of work. She helped me out once, letting me stay with her at her apartment.

Wicked Wanda was a tiny thing, with more balls than most men. She would perform by spanking the men in her audiences. They adored her as she scoffed at them. She was my one real friend I made at work at that time and I was honored to be her Bridesmaid. I don't think the marriage lasted but a few months though. I've lost track of her and Tanya, both of whom I made love to, both of whom I liked. C'est la vie. I hope they have had happy lives. I hope that if they remember me, it is with kindness.

Big Stage

You were the Headliner when you did

a big show

on the Big Stage...

At first I stripped, but the longer I worked for the Brothers, the more elaborate my shows got. Mai Lin and I made a film together, posed with one another for magazine covers and lay-outs, and did a bondage-type strip on the Big Stage. It was indeed the biggest room in the place, big like a movie theater. They would show X-rated films there between floor shows.

Mai-Lin was one of the few Asians in the business and we got along splendidly. She was very pretty and very open to sexual ideas. She loved to get her nipples pinched, even by clothes-pins! So we did an entire act around the clothes-pins on stage.

My very last show on the Big Stage was my "China Girl" show. That was a song by David Bowie and I acquired a fabulous kimono to use as a costume. The kimono was white silk embroidered by golden threads to form golden flying storks and had a red silk lining. I'd appear in this amazing work of art, twirling, dancing. When I took off the huge ornate costume, I could lay upon it comfortably to finish my "floor show." Sorry to be mixing cultures, but it made a fantastic prop.

Being Bipolar

Being bipolar hurt my parents when
I threw tizzies as a kid and complicated
my life long after I'd lived on Polk Street.
Acting-out mania drove most people away
from me. I couldn't easily make girlfriends.
Because of my super sex drive, I went
into the Adult World of magazines, X-rated
movies and stripping on stage. Touring
to many stages across the USA, being
photographed in Europe and making films
in both France and Germany.

I went first to Germany to tour, a dance/appearance. I was to be given a "date" with someone in the audience. The dates were either non-existent or just a brief get-together. The company putting up the money for me to tour with a film of mine put me up in Intercontinental Hotels. The buffets there were huge, full of every sort of meat. Glad to not be a vegetarian while in Germany, I would have starved.

The second trip to Germany I stayed with a famous photographer and his wife. I got really severe jet-lag, but they revived me with blood-orange juice, which I had never tasted before, but loved. It was orange juice, but red, the fruit was grown in Israel. He would photograph me and he and his wife would make love with me.

On my way home I stopped in Paris to meet a man, Francis, who would become my benefactor for another trip to Paris. He put me up at the George V Hotel to meet with him, a glorious, expensive place. My friend Tiffany Clark, who I made movies with, and who stayed at Polk Street, went to Europe quite often to visit with the self-exiled Roman Polanski. She arranged this introduction for me to Francis, my one and only "Sugar Daddy."

My arousal on film was real. Few of the players in erotic films could really act. We were bodies saying lines that were willing to screw on film. There were only a very few of us then as the making of films was illegal. I went to jail in two states (one on the West Coast, one in the East) for being on film having sex. All the people in films, both actors and crew knew one another, but I didn't fraternize with them off set. At home I was throwing manic tantrums - throwing dishes, throwing myself about. Being bipolar feels as though you are always flailing from one situation to the next. You like the pain, want pain to know you are alive.

This kind of "acting" and the stage saved me from being so violent. My mania enraged me and sex could channel this anger. During my film-making, I was also very lonely. Even though married, he would run around on me, as I would also seek gratification elsewhere. We could have been great friends, but sex got in the way to make us enemies. (We did produce a daughter who is a vibrant, smart human being. I thank him for that!)

Enjoying the women at the O'Farrell Theatre, I could make love with them and satisfy my manic drive, and they were my girlfriends of the moment. Lovers at the theatre and at my home, the friendships wouldn't last. Out of these times in the 1970s, only my daughter and Morgan have stuck with me. Thank the Goddess they are in my life. They are two of my favorite people on the planet, along with the Obamas and "my" Paul. My granddaughter would name me "Grandma Serena" and Paul "Grandma's Paul." He is "my" Paul.

I am a Star in a very small pool of celebrity. I don't make the Evening News. Once I was mentioned on the cover of the *San Francisco Chronicle* because of my horrid custody battle.

My first exhibition of collages was reviewed in a half page article in the *San Francisco Chronicle*. The actress Sharon Stone lived with the owner of the newspaper for a time. She and I both helped raise money for AIDS research. Small world, all being connected.

I have been able to keep making some money from my celebrity by writing books and making infrequent Public Appearances. (Seeing my Fans has stopped completely now because of Covid-19.)

So being bipolar has only affected those close to me - my Lovers, Family and my few Friends.

Displaying his Manic Craziness all over the Evening News is Kayne; I feel sorry for him and know medicine could help him. So glad I am not so famous that I were to be embarrassing myself so publicly! I am happy that I've found the right combination of pills that keep me level at last. I wish that all people with this disorder could have help.

Life can be a roller-coaster-like nightmare unless you have medications that level your brain imbalances. I'd had a painful, burning sensation in my solar plexus area - it seemed to be the source of my rage. Medicine took away my anger, fury was like a sore ulcer in my body. I no longer have that painful burning sensation, I do have TD, but that's a very small price to pay for taking medication that helps me.

As with many people, I have started and stopped taking my medications. They feel at first as though they inhibit you, make you less creative. But they don't really "tamp you down" or destroy your creativity. You just need to get adjusted to this new norm. Medication will allow you freedom of expression while maintaining a balance of your up and downs. The ups and downs can be a fun ride, but slinging your being from one pole to the other can be exhausting! Going on and off the medications just means you need to start over each time. My advice is to keep taking the pills, eventually you will like the affect. It does take some time to get used to, however. You are creating a new personality that doesn't need to be manic or depressed. This is indeed a huge change for the better. I tried a few different combinations of pills, and while testing to see what was right for me I gained and lost pounds. I recall ballooning up with one anti-depressant, I was huge!

At our flat on Polk Street, Morgan was learning to speak French - part of why he was so damn hot to me. Speaking French is utterly sexy. You need to use your whole face, your mouth, tongue and vocal cords as a sexual organ. Most Americans don't get this - you need to make love to each word.

Morgan would speak French to me and I'd shiver with pleasure. Everything he did was sexy to me. I'd been starving for real affection and a good lover. A lover who would love me sexually without needing the extremes of fetishes. To me, Morgan resembled my favorite rock singer of all time, Robert Plant, and I'd climax every time I'd hear the rock star sing certain songs - still do! "Way down inside..."

Thanks, "Bob." You were SEX in the 1970s.

After I had met my friend Francis in Paris, we began to plan a month's visit to Paris. Francis was home in the City of Lights alone, as his wife went off in the summer as most Parisians did. New York has an exodus too - people go out of town in the hot weather. (In Paris they have a saying that "it is impossible to find bread in August.")

I told Francis that I'd love to join him, be his Summertime Mistress if I could bring along my child and her Nanny. He agreed with these terms and Morgan boned up on his language skills. Meanwhile, Francis would rent the US Ambassador's daughter's apartment for us. The apartment was lovely, located in a perfect setting, easy to get to the Metro. It was a duplex, furnished by an expert. There were whale tusks in it and it had a large balcony that was pretty private. The furniture was white and new. Lovely, and bedrooms enough to accommodate the three of us.

Francis was surprised my Nanny was male! (Since then, thanks to the TV show *Modern Family* we call them "Mannies" or "Manny's"!)

I made it up to Francis by being a great cock-sucker and friend to him. He took me every night to a more fabulous restaurant where we'd dine for hours on the sumptuous sauces-with-food. At home I lick my plate at the end of a meal, but French fine dining provides you with flat sauce spoons to get every drop.

The first place he took me was on the boat that tours the Seine, the best way to familiarize yourself with the beautiful old city. Francis was Jewish and complained he was bullied by the very Catholic citizens. I gave him a shoulder on which to cry out his woes and my body whenever he wanted it. I was just so happy to have Morgan exploring Paris with Lucy. They went to Museums and to the gardens of the Park and he had a chance to speak French. The French can be snooty about their language because no one can speak it unless they were born to it - but Morgan got along. I had Francis to help, and if I took a cab, I'd write out where I wished to go.

Francis and I would dine out often together, we both loved to eat, and he loved showing off his wealth by showing me off in fancy establishments. We began our meals around 8pm and sometimes be having our cheese and fruit platter (dessert) as late as eleven o'clock. He told me you can always tell an out-of-towner because they were the first seating in a restaurant. Tourists would eat from six 'til eight and be out of the local's way. This was one of the best months of my life. I was wined and dined in the most exquisite city on earth and I got to share it with to my best friends Lucy and Morgan. I gained weight from all the buttery croissants.

I went home to the States to be in the film *Insatiable* with Marilyn Chambers whom I knew from the O'Farrell Theatre, but we'd never been in a movie together. *Insatiable* was her own project and turned out to be quite a good movie. She was a thoroughly sexual creature, somewhat androgynous. Full of explicit fire, she'd use you up! I did my scene with her in a hot tub and she was hot to trot. She was fun, fabulous, very friendly and exuded lust.

Morgan and Lucy would stay overseas, going to various countries. I heard that she got Scarlet Fever while there, which would cause her to have a slight heart murmur. I witnessed her fainting several times when she was an adult in Florida. A favorite book of mine is *Little Women* and I remember Beth getting Scarlet Fever in it.

I recall wiring Morgan money from the big Bank of America on Market Street in San Francisco but I know I didn't send money enough, or often enough.

I, unfortunately, was on drugs, bipolar and couldn't function responsibly - and Morgan wasn't there to help me! Morgan would leave my life for nearly forty years and I've always assumed it was because I left him stranded in Europe. I've regretted my actions towards this incredible man and always hoped he would forgive me. It is a true Miracle that he is back in my life. I praise the Goddess and April and Ashley of *The Rialto Report*.

It was because Morgan wrote about me and posted his photos on *TheRialtoReport.com* that we found each other. I had been interviewed by them before. They are the executors of Jamie's estate. I am so very thankful and honored that Morgan remains my friend. I feel tender about our friendship and I just hope and pray we will always be in touch.

I am now a Grandmother to three kids - all smart and beautiful; of course! I love this new role and love my Lulu even more. I dread that I hurt her by attempting suicide in 2002 - so very sorry, a deep regret. Now that I've lived through that terrible time, I wish only to live. Live for my beautiful daughter and her beautiful children, live for myself and for "my" Paul, live for Art for Art's Sake and live for the day I might meet Morgan in person again.

I love Lucy. I am so proud of Lucy: she is a good person, a wonderful wife and a supercalifragilistic mother. She's overcome the hardships her Mom and Pop put upon her, she is a self-made, fantastic, being. She has learned so much in her life. I am so happy she is my loving daughter.

Afterward

I was a big letter-writer, but that has been replaced electronically. My best childhood memories are of getting "picture letters" from my grandmother, Busha. When she died, she had $12 and boxes and boxes full of pictures she'd cut out for her letters. A box might contain a few, or a lot, of pictures she'd cut out of magazines or greeting cards. Pictures of birds, flowers, poems - anything she thought she'd send on to elaborate her feelings.

Busha would spend literally all day at card shops looking at each card, buying a stack to cut up. This was her art, her hobby, her joy. And to receive a Picture Letter was a joy! They were sprinkled with her love, illustrated. She taught me how fun it is to get a note, how illustrating it can add to your pleasure. Even when emailing, I attach a photo most times. I learned this from Busha. This book is like a Picture Letter from me to you who are reading it. Hope it has brought you Joy!

•

I recently received an email that made me cry. The missive was from Morgan, and lifted so much guilt from my shoulders. He explained that it was not Scarlet Fever, as I'd been told, but Whooping Cough that LuLu had while in Europe with him:

"Lu had Keuchhusten. I remember that German word because I was often purchasing a honey-lemon-herbal cough syrup for her. I actually got pretty good at saying Keuchhusten… It wasn't easy in the beginning. I made a lot of pharmacists laugh - then they were sympathetic ;-)

Lucy with her Grandpa and Teddy.

I was told that whooping cough was, at the time, considered a "childhood disease" and there were no longer vaccines for it. When I noticed the Scarlet Fever reference I took a few minutes to remember. Keuchhusten kept popping up in my memory."

I too got Whooping Cough as a kid. Was not Vaccinated. This year's Vaccination for Covid-19 was my first. I told the doc who gave me "the jab," and he said Whooping Cough was very serious. I must have been a toddler because I remember having it. I recall the whoop from my belly that made it's way up my little body to become a cough that would not stop. Racking coughs, that took my whole body and shook it up!

Vaccinations were not available in Germany at this time, so she suffered, but she got through it. In a weird way I feel closer to her, knowing we went through this same test, and we both came out of it stronger. I probably just didn't think to get her the shot had it been available here in the states.

Lucy and her family are now fully Vaccinated against the world-wide plague, as are Paul and myself. We are looking to have a future!

Cottages at Park Place
        near the Boardwalk.
My child was born there,
        by the beach.
I'm headed for the doctor.

The sky is white with fog, my brain
        filled with white noise.

My brain isn't the same as yours,
        not quite.
Seeing a string of numbers
I cannot read them, I give up.

People demanding more of me,
        I'm astounded.
Haven't I told you all?
I've painted my thoughts
Until my fingers are bleeding.

Why the insistence to form words
that don't say enough, can't speak
the Truth and usually twist me
        into trouble?

www.ingramcontent.com/pod-product-compliance
Lightning Source LLC
Chambersburg PA
CBHW050642150426
42813CB00054B/1158